Life Happens! Now What?

Marvin Robert Wohlhueter

Trilogy Christian Publishers
A Wholly Owned Subsidiary of Trinity Broadcasting Network
2442 Michelle Drive
Tustin, CA 92780

For information, address Trilogy Christian Publishing
Rights Department, 2442 Michelle Drive, Tustin, Ca 92780.
Trilogy Christian Publishing/ TBN and colophon are trademarks of Trinity Broadcasting Network.
For information about special discounts for bulk purchases, please contact Trilogy Christian Publishing.
Manufactured in the United States of America

10 9 8 7 6 5 4 3 2 1
Library of Congress Cataloging-in-Publication Data is available.
ISBN 978-1-63769-876-1
ISBN 978-1-63769-877-8 (ebook)

Author photo provided by Balazs Vizin. To learn more about his offerings as a company, visit his website or call his personal cell: www.cascadecreative.us; Mobile: 470.429.0288

Dedication

The Twins

Elise Grace

Elise Grace came first. She was born at 5:01 a.m. on August 15, 2019. Her lively nature in the NICU won the hearts of all the nurses. Elise was the spirited one in the preemie ward. She always liked to keep the schedule shifting when we would visit her. These past 24 months since her arrival have been magical to me as her Daddy. She has continued to fill my soul with her tender moments and fond affection. I cannot wait to watch her life unfold and see all that God has in store for her. Elise, you are precious in every way. God has called you to be a worship leader for the world. I love you so much, Buttercup.

Josiah Robert

Josiah Robert, technically the younger brother though now much more prominent in size than his sister, was born at 5:02 a.m. on August 15, 2019. Yes, he had one more minute of condo living in his mother's womb. Yet, once he made his entrance to this world, the doctors scrambled to get him stable. Josiah had a challenging beginning with his lungs, as he and his sister, Elise, were born at thirty-two weeks. Two surgeries to his credit at such an early start make him a warrior in my book. He was a sleeper in the NICU for almost forty days with his blue crochet cap.

Nevertheless, he emerged as a hero to all the medical personnel. Today, he is no longer the quiet one. He has guns blazing as his maleness takes off. Josiah, you have a calling on your life to preach the gospel of Jesus Christ. I love you, my little man.

Together, you are bringing so much joy and laughter into our home. Yes, it took ten years for your arrival but was it ever worth the wait. Mommy and Daddy think you mutually hung the moon! You have both had the dubious honor of living through our COVID-19 caper and the unique experience of 2020 as your starting point. We will have many moments to reminisce on the road called life. Life happens! Now what? You can relate well to this theme as your little journey is unfolding.

Thank You

To those who read my writings, I want to thank you and offer wisdom, encouragement, and faith. You have made the clear choice to keep adding to your growth and investing in your spirit. That makes you a star in my book. Why?

Wisdom: The best life to live is one filled with God's wisdom over every circumstance and challenge you face. Think through its benefits and realize its power.

Encouragement: Like oxygen to the human soul, words that offer life are potent and impactful. If you drink these words in with endless opportunity, the result is life-changing.

Faith: No one stumbles into a life of walking with God. The effort to know God, and His ways, is driven by conviction and motivation. Never give up on daily pursuing God and His righteousness.

Look at the above ingredients with the potential each one has over your life. Rate yourself today and increase daily in these critical areas of development.

Table of Contents

CHAPTER ONE

I Did Not See It Coming!

We closed 2019 with a Christmas party in early December. Our adult married couples' group gathered to celebrate the holiday season and reconnect for the first and last time after the birth of our twins. Having met consistently for a year and a half prior, we were out-of-pocket from July of that year until early December. Hence, Lorraine and I felt the need to gather with our couple friends and finish 2019 with an evening of food and fellowship.

During this meeting, I shared a brief devotional with the couples. The critical thrust was this question, "What does 2020 mean in most circles?" As you could imagine, the answers were plenteous, but we all agreed the term was most relevant in the optical world. 20/20 was a standard term in this field. It was in that setting one would hope to have such an outcome with each visit. To have perfect vision would be a win from the time spent with the eye doctor. We all chuckled and understood the parallel of perfect vision in the natural and what it could mean to each life and couple in the spiritual or faith realm.

From this lens or viewpoint, each married patron took some time to offer how they hoped 2020 would play out, personally and as a couple. Each person in the room wanted to meet God uniquely with determination and devotion as the year turned and the new year dawned. Some wanted a better marriage to emerge amid the daily living they walked in. Others wanted less stress and a better handle on life's demands. Still, most individuals agreed that we all needed a touch of God's peace and presence in the coming year. Each heartfelt declaration gripped the engaged audience, and we truly believed that God would show up in such powerful ways, and we availed our lives to Him.

We ended the night with sweet companionship and parted to our respective homes. The thought of 2020, or 20/20, would leave many of our minds. The new year did have our attention, but to say it was fastened to our thought life would be an erroneous statement. Concerned? Sure. Worried? Not on your life! We had seen years come and years go. There was nothing new here, for the most part. Life marches on.

The *it* I am referring to in the title of this chapter is the infamous year 2020. I suspect you did not see it coming either. The whole world stood in wonder at what was happening. The year 2020, start to finish, was marked as the most *unscripted* year in modern history. Those are not my words, but that of the populous. From the global pandemic that ripped through the world and all of the shelter-in-place edicts to the murder of George Floyd, characterized by excessive police brutality and the resulting riots and protests in the streets and the burning of cities around the United States, the year started with colossal hardships. Next, added to this weight was the presidential election, and the subsequent allegations of mail-in ballot fraud, coupled with the legal challenges over who was the truthful winner, have caused many souls to become weary and confused. This election was touted as the most important in the history of the United States' longevity. Yes, you heard that right. We have been a formal nation since 1776, and our 2020 election was declared the most epic one. That alone would be enough to cripple a year, and a people, for that matter.

Undoubtedly, in 2021, our continued days of economic uncertainty as the nation battles on along with the persistent consideration of the COVID-19 crisis and the need to get fully vaccinated, open our country up, and get back to some level of everyday living. As former President Trump has said many times during 2020, "The cure cannot be worse than the disease."[1] Regardless of your political affiliation, that is a fair statement in any audience.

Nevertheless, that was life 2020 style: COVID-19, no professional sports, shutdowns, masks, social distancing, working from home, digital learning for students, massive job losses, George Floyd's death, riots, protests, burning cities, police reform, continued mass shootings, presidential election face-off, mail-in ballot fraud, supreme court battles, and to top it off, a domestic terror explosion on Christmas morning in Nashville, Tennessee. Mama, stop the train. I want to get off the ride. This world has gone crazy. I was shocked in 2020. Guess what? So were you! Who can handle a deluge of funk all at the same time? The influence of all these ingredients has paralyzed society.

As we joyously celebrated Memorial Day weekend in the United States in 2021 and have the ability to spend time with family once again, can we welcome the fact that God still has the final say over our lives today? That is why this book is going to touch the world over with hope, God's hope. Your life's story has an outcome with God's name on it. Why? That is easy! The author of a story always puts *his* name on the book. So, God is authoring your storyline. Now, your accounts details may differ from each person reading this book, but here is the *best* news: Jesus Christ does not change! 2020 did not adjust the Savior of the world. The Bible declares this truth in Hebrews 13:8, "Jesus Christ is the same yesterday and today and forever." Did you catch that last word, forever? Let that sink into your soul and spirit. Jesus Christ is the *unchanging rock*. He is waiting patiently for an invitation into the middle of your life and situation. Jesus Christ will make all the difference in your journey called life, even when you have a year like 2020!

Why? That is an easy answer. He is the "Way maker, miracle worker, promise keeper, and light in the darkness." As the lyric says in "Way Maker", "My God, that is who you are."[2] While the song came out a few years earlier, it seemed to find its wings and make a grand entrance in 2020 as the theme for a year filled with confusion, uncertainty, fear, anxiety, depression, and constant pressure.

Take a few minutes and watch Alexandria's Pentecostal church's version of Way Maker from 2018 on YouTube. That is where I first heard the song. The song touched my life, and no doubt, changed it that day. It can change your life too. *Life Happens! Now What?* This book is a celebration of the ultimate way maker rewriting each story that existed in death's grip to a tale filled with heaven's promise. Hallelujah to the Lamb of God!

Think It Through!

1. What were your aspirations of 2020 before COVID-19 hit?

    _____

2. Where you prepared for what lay ahead in year 2020? How did you respond?

    _____

3. How were you able to adjust your life to navigate your new conditions?

    _____

4. Jesus Christ never changes. Does that bring you hope today?

    _____

5. Jesus Christ is the Way Maker, Miracle Worker, Promise Keeper, and Light in the Darkness. Do you believe that?

    _____

6. Is He your Way Maker? What is your relationship with Him today?

    _____

7. Did 2020 give you 20/20 focus? Why or Why Not?

    _____

Chapter Two

Life Happens! Now What?

No one would deny that life can go sideways at times. We all have to face these types of situations. That is nothing new. I've been there. You have been there. That's life, as they say. Years ago, a bumper sticker came out that said, "Stuff Happens" (or a variation, I'm sure you have seen this sticker, too). While I would not be so bold as to place that on my car due to its offensive language, the claim has a tinge of truth. Stuff happens, and it happens a whole lot, if we are honest. I like to say it this way since I am a student of everyday life, "Life Happens!" That is a little kinder on the ears but just as heavy on the heart. It is those *Life Happens!* moments that rip at the soul of each of us. Yet, if we are honest, we would say that 2020 was a continuous string of unending *Life Happens!* situations.

Can I get an amen to that? It is not that they happened that causes us the most grief. It is the fact that they never let up as one punch landed after another. It is like boxing with an octopus. You have two hands to defend yourself while he has eight. When you think you are protected, another glove comes out of nowhere to land a blow. You get the picture. Punch after punch after punch was what 2020 felt like to most of us.

Friend, I have good information for you. This difficulty is nothing new. Jesus warned us that life would play out like this, "I have told you these things, so that in me you may have peace. In this world, you will have trouble. But take heart! I have overcome the world" (John 16:33). We could all use a good dose of peace in 2021 and beyond. The above verse can be summed up as follows: The world gives trouble, but Jesus gives peace. That is good to know! It is also noteworthy that Jesus Christ can deliver on that *peace* since He overcame death for us and conquered the world.

The second half of this book's title is what gives each of us the most difficulty. Why? Humanity tends to behave like an ostrich and sticks its head in the sand. If we cannot see it, then we do not have to deal with it. Just because you do not see it does not deny it exists.

Now what? has the potential to flip your life. In recent years, the word *flip* has been used everywhere on HGTV. Maybe you have seen *Property Brothers*, *Love it or List it*, and the famous duo of Chip and Joanna Gaines in Waco, Texas. These home renovators have caused us to marvel as the before-and-after shots appear side-by-side. Once in shambles, a renovator with a keen eye can envision a makeover for a home that the current owner never imagined. That is why these transformations speak to our emotions. No one would have believed that a house in ruins could be flipped into a mark of beauty.

Guess What? Your heavenly Father has seen the effects of 2020 on your life. And, with a keen eye for renovation, He plans a restoration project that is out of this world. Yes, God is about to flip your life. The before life will be nothing like your after portrait. Two verses come to mind as I close this chapter. One speaks of a boxing-type image and being in the ring of life as noted in the book of Proverbs 24:16, "for though the righteous fall seven times, they rise again, but the wicked stumble when calamity strikes." If you were reared in the eighties or have seen them on cable television, you are acquainted with the Rocky movies and actor Sylvester Stallone. In the epic final rounds of every fight, Rocky digs deep within to rise and conquer his opponent. You must be willing to do the same in life. Sure, you will get knocked down, but get back up and keep in the fight.

Lastly, there is great comfort because God can make beauty from the ashes of a year like 2020. This thought is echoed in Scripture,

> The Spirit of the Sovereign LORD is on me, because the LORD has anointed me to proclaim good news to the poor. He has sent me to bind up the brokenhearted, to proclaim freedom for the captives and release from darkness for the prisoners, to proclaim the year of the LORD's favor and the day of vengeance of our God, to comfort all who mourn, and provide for those who grieve in Zion—to bestow on them a crown of beauty instead of ashes, the oil of joy instead of mourning, and a garment of praise instead of a spirit of despair. They will be called oaks of righteousness, a planting of the LORD for the display of his splendor.
>
> Isaiah 61:1–3

Wow! By now, you should be shouting for joy. Let your voice be heard in your room, among your family, at your job, and in your circles of influence. God can flip your life, even after a year like 2020. Look at those contrasting words: beauty vs. ashes, joy vs. mourning, praise vs. despair. God will turn it around for you. Never stop believing that. It is your lifeline for *Life Happens!* moments. And the *Now What?* is this final exclamation, "They will be called oaks of righteousness, a planting of the LORD for the display of his splendor" (Isaiah 61:3).

God wants to put your *after* photograph on display for the world to see His wondrous works. No, 2020 does not have the right to declare the end of the story. God does! Let's get to flipping.

Think It Through!

1. Stuff Happens! Have you seen the bumper sticker? Did it speak to you?

   _____

2. My version: Life Happens. Why do you think life is so hard?

   _____

3. Jesus said trouble would be coming your way. What are your plans for trouble coming into your life?

   _____

4. Now What? What actions do you plan to take in light of the events of 2020?

   _____

5. Could God use 2020 to flip your life for the better? Might your 20/20 focus benefit from such a colossal year? How so?

   _____

6. God is in the renovation and restoration enterprise. What stands out to you in the final verses listed?

   _____

7. Beauty vs. Ashes, Joy vs. Mourning, and Praise vs. Despair. How do you think God can make that happen?

   _____

CHAPTER THREE

You've Learned Much – Use It

Life in 2020: the whole shebang came to a screeching halt. From professional sports to church life, student academics, after-school programs, social interaction, work from home, and the like. The year felt like a divine pause button was hit, and all that was moving in our society was mandated to stop. Frozen in time and called to abrupt obedience. While we fought it, we sure needed it.

Why? Simply put, we learned so much about ourselves during this time. Things we never knew! Factors we may have let slip through the cracks due to busyness. Matters we had forgotten about in our life's story. Sadly, we can tend to live on autopilot if we are not careful. Nevertheless, 2020 shook up the apple cart and forced us to evaluate everything about our life's makeup. *Now What?* We must decide how to use our newfound information. Use it or lose it is always true.

If truth be told, we had many forced experiments due to COVID-19. Effects we would have never set out to learn on our own, such as outcomes our employers would not have voluntarily offered us as alternatives to modern work dynamics. Yet, they worked and with a bang. We can never be the same because these new changing aspects proved to be enormous. We have learned too much about life to retreat to business as usual. You have more knowledge about yourself, too. So, the question of the hour is how do you use it for your good in the future? While everyone's story about COVID-19 is different, it did create some universal learning experiences.

For starters, academics for children were done from home. Those of you with children, had a forced homeschooling opportunity thrust into your lap. How did you deal with that? I heard some loved it, and some struggled with the daily demands of teaching. Yet, you got to spend way more time with your kids than ever before. What a plus to build on the relationship with each child? In addition, I am sure your availability blessed your child at a moment's notice: quick access or having to schedule them into your daily planner. What a perk to each relationship! Don't look back to the old way of learning. Even if you return to the classroom someday, please do not miss out on the connection bolstering time moving forward.

Next, our employers sent us home to work out of the corner office or a makeshift one in the spare bedroom down the hall. What started a bit clunky and weird is now a desired commodity in every work setting around the globe. I don't know about you, but I appreciate working from home. I got to see my twins growing daily in the next room as I passed by for coffee or a bathroom break. To make matters even more impressive, my employer learned that our team was more effective from home and sales solutions were at an all-time high. What? No need to monitor the professional in his cubical as a means of productivity. Yes, that has been proven for nearly eighteen months now. With the vaccine in full swing, employers are trying to figure out what to do with employees who successfully keep the business wheels moving while working from home. Let's use what we learned to be more productive as a society in the marketplace. What about your work-from-home experience? You learned about organizational skills, internal motivation, taking good notes, getting back with customers, using zoom technology, and the ease of working remotely, given enough time to master it. As a society, we can't ever go back to being forced to commute to the office and babysitting the professional. I would suggest discussing with your employer about a hybrid work arrangement where both can benefit moving forward.

Thirdly, and this one is a big one, local parishes or churches were closed for worship. I am not assuming you are a person of faith, but if you are, then at some level, you were forced to grow personally during the shutdown. Many learned of their complete dependence on the pastor or priest for their spiritual pep talk or proverbial shot in the arm of inspirational messages to become a better person. We all needed that hope each day.

The word on the street is that online viewing and cable opportunities exploded as people across the planet turned to these means of getting spiritual guidance and encouragement. While I am not advocating you never return to your local place of worship, I suggest you never lose sight of the fact that you must keep growing on your own and allow once-a-week visitation to enhance your spiritual journey and relationship base.

What many learned is there are numerous tools available to grow one's faith. Check out some of the apps for phones that have devotional plans. Get reading materials from your favorite author and commit to fifteen to thirty minutes per day to stretch your thinking and enlarge your heart. While prayer may not be a routine in your daily schedule, it only takes five to ten minutes, at a minimum, to share your soul with your Creator. Ventilating the heart through the mind and out the mouth creates great healing and, ultimately, wholeness in body, mind, and spirit.

> A good man out of the good treasure of his heart brings forth good; and an evil man out of the evil treasure of his heart brings forth evil. For out of the abundance of the heart his mouth speaks.
>
> Luke 6:45 (NKJV)

As a pastoral counselor, I can let you in on a bit of a secret. If you don't allow the heart to ventilate through the mouth, the contaminated areas will continue to grow and fester. It would be best to clean the soul through communication with a pastor, priest, lay counselor, trusted friend, or accountability partner. It is vital to your health and wellbeing. Keep doing this desired practice along with all the other means of building your faith muscle.

A fourth ingredient that got interrupted was our socialization schedules. For many, the shelter-in-place edict felt like solitary confinement in a prison cell. To be cut off from everyday living was like a knife through the heart of our being. We are wired for relationships, and we were being told to shut them all down, at least for a time. No face-to-face interaction was the mandate, not even with immediate family. Yet, what emerged was life-changing. I had never heard of the word *Zoom* before on the internet. I bet you had not either.

Nevertheless, Zoom meetings are now an ordinary part of reality, like breathing. If we are honest, it is fantastic to use. You can even share computer screens. Gather dozens of people for a group discussion, as we are with a men's small group with participants from California, North Carolina, Georgia, Florida, and the West Indies. That's right, every other Saturday, I share my first book: *My Life Is: Real vs. Ideal.* This technology is a game-changer for social interaction and relationship building. Yet, pre-pandemic, most never knew of its existence. How do you use Zoom technology today? Could you ever go back to not using it?

Friend, these are just four of the many areas impacted by COVID-19. What else is for the better because of this forced shutdown? Is your schedule tamer these days? Less running around? Driving here or commuting there? What about trips to your children's sporting events, piano lessons, karate practice, or after-school programs or activities. What have you done with the massive hours of free time gained from the lack of professional sports on cable television? Here is a kicker: Did you and your spouse get more time together over the past eighteen months? What was the benefit to your marital story? Maybe it showed areas that need improvement. That still helps in the grand scheme of things. Maybe, you took each other for granted before COVID-19, and now you have become best friends again. Use this new way of building bonds of love.

As we land the plane on this chapter, think of what you learned about yourself, and the world, as a result of COVID-19 and its outcomes in 2020. Yes, tens of thousands of deaths are horrific, and I do not minimize the truth of this devilish virus. However, to ignore how you have grown personally and professionally would be unfair to this time of trial.

You've Learned Much – Use It

"Brothers and sisters, I do not consider myself yet to have taken hold of it. But one thing I do: Forgetting what is behind and straining toward what is ahead, I press on" (Philippians 3:13–14).

Press on! Can you do that? Learn from the past. Use it to better you in the present. Anticipate a glorious future as you master the skills and knowledge learned during this COVID-19 season. *Use it.*

Think It Through!

1. COVID-19 forced many experiments on us. What were your top two?

   _____

2. What did you learn about yourself while juggling so many life demands?

   _____

3. What relationships improved during the COVID-19 season and shutdown?

   _____

4. How did your work life change during the shelter-in-place edict?

   _____

5. What do you have in place to vent the heart and share your struggles with another?

   _____

6. Use it or lose it? Those are your options. How do you plan to keep it alive?

   _____

7. Press on! Can you let go of the past and lean into the future with what you have learned about yourself. Yes or no? How will you execute this action?

   _____

CHAPTER FOUR

Your Family Is Closer – Foster It

When a heavenly shutdown occurs, where no one is permitted to venture out of your home except for extreme emergencies, environments change. I suspect your home and family life got the most impacted by the COVID-19 virus. Why? You were mandated to stay indoors and interact only with your immediate family. That would sound delightful in any other context, but a forced shelter-in-place may not leave you feeling warm and fuzzy. Yet, the personal stories that I have heard and experienced all echo the same thing. "Our family is closer than ever before. The depth of our love and devotion to each other is at an all-time high. I would not trade this for anything."

The fact of the matter is that your family was living on relational fumes. Yes, you were in proximity to each other, but the amount of quality, meaningful interactions was scarce. It just goes to prove that you can live under the same roof and see each other every day yet be relatively shallow in the amount of knowledge and understanding you have concerning a family member. In large, children were desperate for their parent's complete affection, a warm embrace, a listening ear, and spirited concern. On the flip side, parents never had discretionary time to foster such an essential relationship with each child. The hustle and bustle of life is a robber of such needs in the spirit of each child.

The fallout of pre-pandemic days was anorexic homes where the souls of each inhabitant were left to find fulfillment in unhealthy places. Indeed, God intended the house to be the safest, most important, and most rewarding place. Nonetheless, your pace of life did not jive with the tempo needed to bolster loving relationships and significant encounters. The challenge you face today is admitting that life was spinning out of control and that it took a global pandemic and a forced shutdown to open up space to see the obvious. That is truly sad but be thankful that awareness finally came to the rescue. No doubt, many bad things have surfaced as a result of a worldwide pandemic.

Nevertheless, can you say that something good occurred out of it in the relational sphere? It is okay to say so. I know it did for me and my home. If you are honest, that relational strain also played out in the most significant relationship of all: Your marriage! Sadly, busyness is a destroyer of marital bliss. You and your spouse had fallen victim to life's demands. It is like trying to hold a tiger by the tail. You are doing your best to stay attached and engage in the moments that occur. Yet, the reality is this: daily needs gobble up your time, and lasting love does not blossom in a microwave setting. When you were courting each other, you dropped hours, daily, for love to flourish.

For many, the forced interaction and closed-door living revealed ripples and wrinkles that needed to be ironed out. That is natural and required. When life is flying by, you keep doing just enough to get by relationally with your mate. You do not see the need to alter or correct some things as unfavorable. We all have issues. You are perfectly normal here.

Suppose the challenges at hand are harder to navigate together personally. In that case, you may even need to see a pastor or counselor but get the necessary assistance required to improve your marriage. Friend, that is not something to be ashamed of doing. Get the help and build on the love you have for each other. It is worth it as your children need Mom and Dad in love and connected in the home. This security in the home environment is more real during an international pandemic than ever before. The world is changing around us.

Let me share a quick story that illustrates this very point. As noted earlier, my wife and I waited almost ten years to have children together. I had two older, adult children from my previous marriage. Our challenges to start a family were real, painful, and almost fatal. Yet, God, in His graciousness, allowed us to have a set of twins finally. Lorraine and I were delighted to begin our family journey. I was fifty-five years old, and my wife was forty-five. We were no spring chickens, as the numbers declare. Nonetheless, the journey has been beautiful, and we are so blessed to have them.

Here is the funny part of the story. The twins are now eating from their high chairs, and, at two years old, this experience can be a taxing one. One day, Lorraine and I were standing in the kitchen, and the twins, Josiah and Elise, were feeding themselves breakfast with their hands. You could surmise that our lives are hectic during this season. While the twins were munching away, I reached over to my beloved and gave her a big hug and a gentle kiss on the cheek. In this moment of fondness, affirming my love for my wife and the wonder of our home, both children stopped chewing to peak at our affectionate encounter. Lorraine and I did not know they were staring at us. When we finally caught wind that we were being investigated for public displays of affection, we turned toward the inquisitive twins. Little did we know that they were both grinning from ear to ear.

My son, Josiah, smiled at us for thirty seconds to a minute. He was spellbound. Josiah approved of such warmness and tenderness at that moment. Why? Even at twenty-four months old, your children are aware of when genuine love is present and growing. It melted my heart to know that Lorraine and I were building a foundation of love, even in these moments of diapers, feeding disasters, crying toddlers, and yes, COVID-19. It is so worth it.

Let me make one other observation about this family time. Because COVID-19 forced us underground, we were only able to invest in our immediate family. Now, I am not against grandparents, aunts and uncles, cousins, and nearby relatives. God created the family unit, and it has magnificence and potential. However, I wonder, in the effort to give ample time to your extended family, you are minimizing the time required to sustain your own? I am certainly not trying to heap guilt on you or cause confusion. What I want you to see is that COVID-19 created unique circumstances that benefited the family in amazing ways. Do not lose sight of that in a rush to get back to normal. You cannot afford to unravel your family's blessings with a quest to feel freedom again.

Your Family Is Closer – Foster It

Create a list of all the positive outcomes of your family's upgraded time during the lockdown. Be specific! What did God show you about the need for more meaningful time with each child? Who would have gotten lost in the shuffle if God did not permit a holy pause in everyday life's demands? Foster your family time as never before. Resist the need to jump into soccer mom schedules, piano recitals, travel sports teams, and other time grabber activities.

Build on what you created during COVID-19 downtimes. I can assure you of this: your children don't want to lose you again to life. Let them see the affection you have for your spouse. Give them glimpses of true love growing in your home. Time is the only natural gift you can give another human being that outlasts the moment. Give your time free from this point forward. Do not squander it, but rather invest it for relational dividends. No one loses when lives are enriched.

Let this verse speak to your soul as a mate: male and female, from Ephesians 5:33, "However, each one of you [husbands] also must love his wife as he loves himself, and the wife must respect her husband."

May love and respect be flowing in your home in abundance these days. Both are vital to a healthy, functioning marriage. For the parents and children, support each other

> Children, obey your parents in the LORD, for this is right. "Honor your father and mother"—which is the first commandment with a promise— "so that it may go well with you and that you may enjoy long life on the earth." Fathers, do not exasperate your children; instead, bring them up in the training and instruction of the LORD.
>
> Ephesians 6:1–4

Together, the bonds of love can ignite creativity, and creativity can be the pathway to everlasting hope. Hope is in short supply these days, but God is the producer of hope that never goes out of style or diminishes. The Bible states in Hebrews 6:19 (NKJV), "This hope we have as an anchor of the soul, both sure and steadfast, and which enters the Presence behind the veil," Allow hope in the Lord to be the anchor that provides safety for your children and marriage. Guard it with your life!

Think It Through!

1. Would you say that your family is closer than ever before? How would you describe it today?

___

2. Relational fumes. Is that an accurate description of your care for each other before COVID-19? What do you plan to do to change that outcome?

___

3. How would you rate your relationship with each child? 1 is low and 10 is high.

___

4. Did your time spent with each child increase during the shutdown? What has been the best part?

___

5. If you are married, did your relationship with your spouse improve during the shelter in place? How?

___

6. Is pastoral counseling something you would consider, if needed? Why?

___

7. Creating safety in the home is not optional. How are you protecting this sacred trust?

___

CHAPTER FIVE

God Is More Intimate – Grow It

This chapter is not meant to freak you out or make you close the book and never pick it back up again. It is always a risk to touch on the God question. I can sense that as I write this chapter. Please keep in mind that you are in control of your choices, and there is never any intention on my part to put pressure on your faith choices or religious view. However, I must at least acknowledge that during this COVID-19 concern, we were quick to see our helplessness in times of crisis. As much as we want to believe we are invincible, we learned the hard way that humans are finite beings. We don't hold all the answers to the world's problems and most significant needs. When the COVID-19 hit and people were dying left and right worldwide, there had to be thoughts of the divine.

How do I know this for sure? That answer can be found in fact, as the online viewing of church services sky-rocketed each week during the lockdown. I also watched Trinity Broadcasting Network one evening, and the host said their rating numbers are off the charts over any other time in history, including 9/11. Google searches of the end times and biblical prophecy are at an all-time high. It is no wonder that people are scared, concerned, aware, and listening. Yes, they are engaged in what the Bible says about all this.

I promise this will be a short chapter to make you more comfortable. Nonetheless, I must ask, has God become more intimate and personal to you? I want to share a passage from the Bible to ponder. It can be found in Proverbs 3:5–6, "Trust in the LORD with all your heart and lean not on your own understanding; in all your ways submit to him, and he will make your paths straight."

Let's take a few minutes and look at two S-words that jump out of the page. The first is *submit*, and the second is *straight*. Allow me to share a life formula with you: *trust + understanding + submission = straightening*. The truth of the matter is this thought, *You are trusting in something, and you are gaining understanding somewhere*. What you must ask yourself is this: Will it sustain you during times of calamity like a global pandemic? I can assure you that our human weakness shows itself real quick when we come up short for answers to this worldwide killer and other life-challenging situations. When life is bearing down, and you are at the end of yourself, where do you go for answers and lasting hope? Wrestle it down. This question must be answered.

This intimate walk with a loving God leads to the first S-word you agree to act on. Submit is not a popular word today in any culture. Why? If you are open to the truth, you admit that calling the shots is what most people like to do. Hardly do we give it a thought that God might have a better way to live our lives. No, we think we are masters of our destiny and march forward to orchestrate every event and circumstance in our lives. How is that working for you? You will come up short every time, and that is the frustrating part. You cannot control everything!

A first cousin to the word *submit* is another S-word. This word is *surrender*. Sadly, society and the devil have hijacked the idea of surrendering as a sign of weakness. Surrender evokes soldiers waving the white flag in defeat and submitting to capture by enemy forces. This version of surrender means being kept alive but dying inside to freedom and dreams. Fact check: Society has lied to you once again. In God's economy, surrender means giving God access to your heart and life. It is not a sign of weakness but a point of entry for the Creator of your soul.

When you settle the argument of who is in complete control of your life, you or God, surrender is no longer a defeat. Instead, it is giving back control of your life's story to God. God owned it first as your Creator. Then, sin stole it through the devil's trickery. Jesus Christ purchased it back from the devil by dying on a cross for the sins of humanity. Now, God wants it given back to Him, but voluntarily as one surrenders their life to Christ. Yes, surrender is a pathway to freedom. Once you have surrendered to God, then the word *submit* is not offensive but rather conducive to a glorious future in Christ Jesus. What could be better?

In marketing, benefits sell every item on the planet, from the iPhone to Amazon Prime. The same is true for the follower of Jesus Christ. What are the benefits of surrender and submission? You guessed it: a straight path. I don't know about you, but life is too short to be wandering through it with no clear sense of direction or purpose. What a waste of your potential. Straight paths can garner magnificent outcomes for God's glory and your good.

As we come to a close on this chapter, has the global pandemic brought you closer to God? Be transparent! If it has, then you should nurture it. If your closeness to God has not changed, reread the scripture listed above. Would the opportunity to have straight paths appeal to you? Have you been drifting through life without a divine rudder to guide you? Or is this more appealing to you?

God Is More Intimate – Grow It

Rick Warren said it best in *The Purpose Driven Life*, "You are as close to God as you choose to be."[3] Life is uncertain, and God is certain. The choice is yours. God longs for you to know Him and pursue Him.

Think It Through!

1. Did the pandemic change your thoughts about God and spiritual matters?

2. Did you Google end times or Bible prophecy? Why or why not?

3. Do you find it hard to trust in the Lord? How about with all your heart?

4. Understanding? What is your source for answers to life's challenges?

5. "In all your ways." Does that seem near impossible to fulfill?

6. *Submit.* Do you struggle to give up the reins of your life to God's control?

7. Straight paths. Does that sound desirous to the human soul? Why?

Chapter Six

Your Schedule Is Slower – Sustain It

Overcrowded, overloaded, and living with no personal margin! Would that be an accurate description of your pre-COVID-19 days? Fatigue could be found in most of our daily lives before the pandemic hit. Why? We are prone to run our lives like we are little machines. Yet, even working machines have scheduled downtimes for preventative maintenance and servicing. Sadly, in the United States and worldwide, we do not praise rest, restoration, and resetting our souls daily. Instead, busyness is a badge of honor to wear and pushing the limits of activity celebrated. What is the outcome? Lives of exhaustion, physical ailments, mental strain, relational brokenness, and spiritual lethargy are the penalties for this unscripted standard of conduct. In short, your body, soul, and spirit get robbed of their created outcome. Is this way of life dangerous? You bet it is! It has casualties at every level of society.

Nevertheless, we march on, ignoring the warnings from our bodies and, even more, our Creator. So, while God did not create the pandemic, God used it to administer a forced retune. Think about it this way. The world came to a dramatic halt! From Wall Street to Washington, from the professional sports world to the local academic world, God permitted a divine pause to include every type of activity in between. No, COVID-19 was not God's master plan for a colossal shutdown. However, He uses it for our good and alters our lives as they presently exist. Why? We, as humans, would never have even considered such a need, much less acted on it. Would you agree?

Let us make this more personal for you. What were your pre-pandemic schedule demands? Dial-in at this moment. Think it through. Were your days a blur of after-school activities like piano lessons, karate practice, school sports teams, and other soccer mom antics? Dad, were you at the office chasing the corporate dream and giving your family the leftovers of your emotional best? Students, what was your daily social media intake and consumption? Who had the most of your time on any given day? What about on the weekends? Did travel ball teams keep you on the go? Maybe, you had a boat, and the nearby lake was calling your name every chance it got. If we fail to trim back the calendar on our own, God sometimes steps in and creates a heavenly do-over of our lives and purpose. Could it be that we were heading for a crash, and God, in His mercy and grace, gave us this time to hit the reset button on our lives? Something for you to think about and ponder.

Why was it so important for God to interrupt your world? Jesus said it best

> Come to Me, all you who labor and are heavy laden, and I will give you rest. Take My yoke upon you and learn from Me, for I am gentle and lowly in heart, and you will find rest for your souls. For My yoke is easy, and My burden is light.
>
> Matthew 11:28–30 (NKJV)

One translation of the Holy Bible uses the words weary and burdened (NIV). Let us put all four words together from both translations for impact: labor, heavy-laden, weary, and burdened. Oddly enough, I found the synonyms for weary as tired, exhausted, drained, and fatigued while writing this text. Interesting! Next, I looked up the synonym for burdened, and it was the word: loaded.

Are you getting the picture, and is that picture describing your life before the global shutdown occurred? Friend, do not feel guilty or condemned. This revelation is an awareness flash. You would not be alone if you experienced these types of words at the core of your soul. Yet, even back in the Bible times, Jesus was mindful that human beings have the propensity to work themselves into the ground and have nothing left but a shell of an existence. That is not God's best for your life. Never has been and never will be.

What is the remedy for this destructive path? Take the world's yoke off your life and put on Jesus' yoke! Stop living for a bigger audience and start living for an audience of one: *Jesus Christ.* Let Him be your example to follow. Why? Because He promises that His "yoke is easy and [His] burden is light" (Matthew 11:30). What is the splendid outcome of this obedient step: "and you will find rest for your souls" (Matthew 11:29). Sold! The most significant remedy for a life of exhaustion is a soul that is at rest.

Modern psychology says that the soul has three integral components: mind, will, and emotion. That offers more explanation for this gain. Think of it this way: mind rest, will rest, and emotional rest. Oh, my goodness! What would life be like for you if your mind no longer keeps racing with random thoughts of negativity and confusion? How about knowing that your life has *meaning, value, and purpose,* the MVP life, and the will inside of you can be settled in God's rest? The final installment of this divine rest would be in the emotions. How amazing it would be to have emotional rest! You heard that right. Your feelings could be experiencing a heavenly calm that would be so relaxing to daily living.

Contemplate this new reality available to you. Maybe, just maybe, God used COVID-19 to get your attention on a better way of doing life for yourself, your marriage, your children, and your home. Slowing down is healthy, holy, and harmonious. Do not go back to the grind. *Ever.*

Your Schedule Is Slower – Sustain It

Take a few minutes and answer the question, who has benefited from this slower pace of life? That is a fair question and much needed as we get back to some normalcy in 2021. Be prayerful about what will be pushing you to resume business as usual. Would it be worth it to move in that direction? Protect what you have and walk in the rest you have found due to a worldwide pandemic and shelter-in-place mandates.

One last thought. Not everyone will applaud your decision to maintain a slower way of life. I can assure you that many will earnestly seek to draw you back into the rat race if they can. Keep your eyes on the prize of tranquility, ease, and enjoyment. The slower life creates the environment for love to grow and flourish. A hectic pace only stifles the ability to engage and listen to the hearts and souls of each family member. In addition, the calmer existence allows God's still, small voice to be heard. More likely, the soul has promptings from God when receptivity to the quiet clamoring representatives of society is turned off. Keep that in view! Let's end with this passage again. Commit this to memory and live in its promise.

> Come to Me, all you who labor and are heavy laden, and I will give you rest. Take My yoke upon you and learn from Me, for I am gentle and lowly in heart, and you will find rest for your souls. For My yoke is easy, and My burden is light.
>
> Matthew 11:28–30 (NKJV)

Think It Through!

1. How would you describe your pre-pandemic way of living?

   _____

2. Busyness – Does the pace of life rob you of quality living? How?

   _____

3. God allowed a divine pause. How did you receive it?

   _____

4. Jesus offers a rest for your soul. Does that sound inviting? What would that mean to you?

   _____

5. Many words define weary: tired, exhausted, fatigued, drained – Do you want out of this way of living? Where would you start?

   _____

6. Jesus' way of life is easy. How is your way of living? Do you want His instead?

   _____

7. Why would others want you to live a hectic pace if it leaves you hollow inside?

   _____

Do you want a permanent change?

_____

CHAPTER SEVEN

Your Dream Is Alive – Pursue It

When COVID-19 was in full swing, life was all over the map. Stability was scarce, and uncertainty was at a record high. Many were losing jobs, houses, finances, and purpose. Initially, some were holding on to the belief that life would bounce back, and this would all be one bad nightmare that would ultimately run its course. Eventually, COVID-19 would be over, and we would shake off the memory from our conscious world and get back to normal. As weeks turned into months and months turned into a year and a half of struggle, the reality of this funk began to make a long-lasting impression on our beings.

Life would be forever changed for the vast majority of people. If there was an excellent outcome of this tragic story, it was that many began to exclaim, "Life is too short!" I do not want to return to my routine. I want to pursue my dreams and personal interests. *What do I have to lose?* was the mantra of the day. Many had lost so much already that they were starting from scratch. With this new condition in full view, they would craft the rest of their storyline differently. I applaud their steadfast spirit!

I read of one career-oriented mother in the fashion industry who lost her job due to COVID-19 when the ability to enter the marketplace was halted. This loss of her income, along with her eighteen years of tenure, caused her to question her aspirations moving forward. She made a career shift and followed her spirit to do something different with her life. I can assure you that she is not alone in her prognosis of the current state of affairs. Many are doing the same thing.

When life goes sideways as this season has, you are more likely to take risks because how could things get worse if you fail? You say, "At the very least, I am going to live out my dreams and desires moving forward." Consequently, the rewards are great as well. When you look at the nature of risk and reward, they are two sides to the same coin. Whether you believe it or not, your life has always been a continued story of risk and reward. Yet, when there is too much to lose, you tend to play it safe and steady. Why? Because you like the life you have created and the consequences of losing this style of living would be too painful. Enter COVID-19, shelter-in-place edicts, forced homeschooling, work-from-home mandates, and no social interaction, to name a few of life's new storylines. You surmise, "What have I got to lose now? My whole world has been turned upside down. Let's make this dream happen!"

Risk much, much reward. Risk little, little reward. No risk, no reward. My dear reader, I am not telling you to throw caution to the wind and go for it, but maybe God is using this COVID-19 season to redirect your future to achieve dreams buried deep in the soul of your being that you would have never risked acting upon. Nevertheless, *now* you are willing to take a step of faith into the unknown with the help of a known God and live out your vision of a new life.

I love it. So, does God! Why? You were created with a divine purpose. You are a one-of-a-kind person with a unique imprint for society's needs. Yes, God crafted your existence to solve one of the many problems our world faces today. Your dream life may be the answer to one of humanity's ills. Playing it safe, while it has its perks, can never give flight to the human experience. Go for it! The rewards will be out of this world, literally.

Can I share my story about pursuing dreams to help illustrate this chapter? I think it will provide insight to you. My degree in mechanical engineering since 1988 has served me well for over thirty years. Yet, concurrently, I have always wanted to do ministry work and inspire others to live for God. These two career paths seemed never to merge. In August 2019, I released my first book. I sensed in my spirit that God wanted me to influence the world over with my writing. Nevertheless, I was still an engineer by day. How would my dream unfold?

In January 2020, God pricked my heart to begin to get up at 5:00 a.m., two hours before my engineering world would kick in, and write books on life, inspiration, and Godly living. It came as a result of reading the following

> To the angel of the church in Philadelphia write: These are the words of him who is holy and true, who holds the key of David. What he opens no one can shut, and what he shuts no one can open. I know your deeds. See, I have placed before you an open door that no one can shut.
>
> Revelation 3:7–8

God prompted me to step through the open door that no man can shut. Your dream is the same way! If God has given you a desire to pursue another career, place to live, business to open, or mission to participate in, then *go for it*. You are standing before an open door, just as I was. Now let me preface this statement with this thought. Yes, I was still working as an engineer Monday through Friday. However, I no longer waited until conditions were perfect to live out my dream. I aspired to be an author, writing materials that encourage others to live for God and carry out their calling in life. Today, this morning, as I am writing this chapter, I am living out my dream. You are the recipient of my willingness to step through the open door. Maybe this authorship will be a full-time gig one day, but why should I wait until that condition arises to fulfill my dream? Do you get my point?

What is your dream? What circumstances are you waiting on the be perfect before you step through the open door? There will never be the best time to start anything noteworthy. I can promise you that. Nonetheless, you can begin to live out your calling and purpose by stepping through the open door. COVID-19 has caused many of us to realize that life is way too short to do something you dread or find unfulfilling each day. While you may not quit your day job, you can begin to launch into the future you long to create.

For me, that was becoming a published author and keynote speaker. Starting small is not a death sentence. It is a launching pad for more extraordinary things. What about you? What can you do today to move in the direction of your dreams? This global shutdown has given you time to process those thoughts. Nurture them and pursue them. Take a risk, get a reward. You have nothing to lose and the world to gain. It will be worth it. Live with no regrets in life.

Your Dream Is Alive – Pursue It

Here is what I suggest doing every week. Get a blank journal, and write down what would be the ultimate dream life for you. If money were no concern and you knew you could not fail, how would that open door look? Have you ever given it this much thought? You must for it to be considered enough to become a reality for you. Next, ask yourself this question, "What can I do today to begin to move in the direction of my dreams?" No, your life will not roll back like the Red Sea to give you a clear walking path. Yes, you will face opposition that will make you want to stop you in your tracks.

Delays will happen. Schedules will shift. Hope, sometimes, gets thin. However, a dream worth pursuing can overcome every obstacle and see them as opportunities to be more than a conqueror.

For me, that was getting up at 5:00 a.m. to write every day. Could I enjoy more sleep? I sure could. Yet, I needed to make some concessions if my dream mattered more to me than the challenges preventing its reality. *It would be best if you did the same.* Be stubborn about the future you want to have. It will not magically appear like a ripe red apple to be picked. Dreams take diligence and persistence to materialize. You need grit and resolve to give it your all for this outcome.

Thirdly, spend fifteen minutes per day in quiet meditation. Clear your schedule and simply think about your dream. God wants you to live out of your capacity, not your scarcity. Yet, unless you hear from Him daily, you will be like a ship without a rudder drifting along on the waters of life. Dreams take laser focus, and you need that kind of clarity every day. Journal your thoughts from this fifteen-minute exchange with God. It will serve you well as you keep stepping through the open doors.

Finally, realize that an oak tree started as an acorn. Likewise, every harvested fruit started as a seedling. Do not overlook this principle. Everything that has ever been created started as a thought, a seed, if you will. Nothing significant in output began any other way. So, your dreams will have to grow organically and over time. There is no fast track to dynamic ambitions. They are fulfilled day by day. Your aspirations are no different. With that said, first, focus on the accomplishments and give thanks to God. Next, focus on the obstacles and spend moments praying to God, who can guide and direct you every step of the way.

Yes, COVID-19 shut down the world as we knew it. However, the emerging world will be full of entrepreneurs who finally stepped through the open door into a new God-sized reality. What a way life can flip for one's good. Enjoy it to the fullest. Good things can emerge from a season of pain and difficulty. Be bold yet humble. Lean into your capability and give it everything you've got. Your dreams make this world a better place. Live them! Glory to God!

Think It Through!

1. Has COVID-19 changed your thoughts about pursuing your dreams? What would you aspire to do?

2. Risk vs. Reward – What is your risk quotient on a scale of 1 (low) to 10?

3. Would the reward be worth it to you to invest in your dreams, despite the unknown? How can God help to fulfill your dreams?

4. The Open Door – God is calling you to a step of faith. How will you respond?

5. Dream Big. Start Small! What can you do today to head toward your dreams?

6. An audience of One! Does God see what you do in the secret moments? What affect does that have on your life?

7. Are you willing to journal your thoughts weekly? What can you learn about yourself during this season?

Can you invite God into this vision?

Chapter Eight

Your Hope Is Only in God – Trust It

When the pandemic hit the globe in early 2020, everyone was clamoring for *hope*. What made this time so scary was that this was a worldwide virus. The entire sphere of humanity was being attacked. When one's health is challenged, there is an awareness of our finite nature. As much as we like to think we are invincible as a people, COVID-19 proved we are dependent on something greater than ourselves, a higher power of sorts. As the death toll climbed with rapid succession, this reality screamed at our frail nature as a society. Yes, we may have invented the iPhone and the internet and traveled to the moon and back. All of these are noteworthy. Useful? Sure! Raised to the ranks of deity or the divine? Hardly! In all of our accomplishments, we can celebrate the brilliance of humankind. Nevertheless, when we reach the end of ourselves during this shutdown season, you and I had better secure our lives on something proven.

This need for security raises the question, "Where do you go to find lasting *hope*?" A proven hope has stood the test of time through world wars, epic natural disasters, nations rising and falling, and a global pandemic that is spinning out of control. Friend, I hear what you are saying, "He is talking about God. I am not a religious person, nor do I believe in organized religion. That faith thing is not for me." You may even be tempted to skip the contents of this chapter. You have every right to do so if you choose. While I cannot make you finish reading my thoughts here, it does not necessarily make the question irrelevant. So, let me ask it one more time, "Where do you go to find lasting *hope*?"

Many think about spiritual matters the closer they get to the end of their days. This ideology would be natural and necessary as life seems to slip through our proverbial fingers. However, that is until an international pandemic, like no other, comes knocking on your heart's door and upsets the whole of life. Please do not see this as meddling. I do care about your life and its outcome. As a student of life, I know that hope is the oxygen that fuels the soul. If you have no hope, then you will live as a shell of a person in no time. No, you may not choose to end your life physically, but you would decide to end your life emotionally in many ways. This realism grips my being for you. Why? Because life is meant to be so much more. You were made for greatness.

God created your story to be a best-seller. A heroic thriller for all to read. Yet, without hope, you check out on life as you know it. You can call it auto-pilot if you like, but it is worse than that. Here is why: You have passengers on your plane! As you navigate your journey, you are taking passengers with you. Your wife and your children are depending on you to arrive safely and at the correct destination. What does it mean for them if your hope quotient hovers around one or two on a scale of ten? Your family can see it in your eyes and feel it as they interact with you. Your passion is gone, and life becomes fillers of time, all marching toward a sad goodbye and a ride in a hearse.

I want to share a series of verses that all speak of hope: God's hope. Let these truths sink deep into the recesses of your mind and soul. Let's begin

> Guide me in your truth and teach me, for you are God my Savior, and my hope is in you all day long.
>
> Psalms 25:5

Why, my soul, are you downcast? Why so disturbed within me? Put your hope in God, for I will yet praise him, my Savior and my God.

Psalms 42:5

Yes, my soul, find rest in God; my hope comes from him.

Psalms 62:5

Blessed are those whose help is the God of Jacob, whose hope is in the LORD their God.

Psalms 146:5

Do any of the worthless idols of the nations bring rain? Do the skies themselves send down showers? No, it is you, LORD our God. Therefore our hope is in you, for you are the one who does all this.

Jeremiah 14:22

...and I have the same hope in God as these men themselves have, that there will be a resurrection of both the righteous and the wicked.

Acts 24:15

And hope does not put us to shame, because God's love has been poured out into our hearts through the Holy Spirit, who has been given to us.

Romans 5:5

May the God of hope fill you with all joy and peace as you trust in him, so that you may overflow with hope by the power of the Holy Spirit.

Romans 15:13

Remember that at that time you were separate from Christ, excluded from citizenship in Israel and foreigners to the covenants of the promise, without hope and without God in the world.

Ephesians 2:12

Command those who are rich in this present world not to be arrogant nor to put their hope in wealth, which is so uncertain, but to put their hope in God, who richly provides us with everything for our enjoyment.

I Timothy 6:17

...in the hope of eternal life, which God, who does not lie, promised before the beginning of time...

Titus 1:2

God did this so that, by two unchangeable things in which it is impossible for God to lie, we who have fled to take hold of the hope set before us may be greatly encouraged.

Hebrews 6:18

While you may or may not believe the Holy Bible as accurate or the inspired word of God, you cannot deny that there are many references to *hope* in Scripture. Guess what? I did not reference and list every occurrence to hope in the Bible. I can assure you that the Word of God is a book about hope, from the table of contents to the maps at the end of God's story. Hope is the primary theme of Scripture. *Why*, you may wonder?

In this season, we are facing a large-scale pandemic. Notice, this is upgraded from the much-used word: epidemic. No! You could not use that word here for this outcome. I never used the phrase pandemic in a sentence before COVID-19. Truthfully, I had never even heard the word before. I suspect you had not either. Not anymore. It is common vocabulary in 2021 and for the rest of our natural days.

I need lasting hope because pandemics exist. It would be best if you had everlasting hope also because pandemics live. Today this knowledge may be the tip of the spear, but that does not mean things cannot worsen in modern living. They can, and they do. There might not be news coverage on it, but devastating things happen in your home and your world that need hope to overcome. Therefore it is paramount that the potential to be disappointed is eliminated no matter where you place your eternal hope.

No, I did not say minimized, downscaled, or marginal in its effects. The only acceptable standard for hope is that it can never be eliminated from your realm. Otherwise, it is no hope at all. Who can deliver such hope in a fallen world? Think through your options carefully. While you may not be a Bible thumper, and I can accept your decision to choose your life course, I want to ask one last time the question, "Where do you go to find lasting *hope*, one that will not disappoint in any season and for any reason? Search the globe over for sources of this kind of hope. I find only one: Jesus Christ, as noted in the Word of God. This kind of hope does not let you down.

> Kings will be your foster fathers, and their queens your nursing mothers. They will bow down before you with their faces to the ground; they will lick the dust at your feet. Then you will know that I am the LORD;

those who hope in me will not be disappointed.

Isaiah 49:23

Not only can God's Word make such an ambitious claim, but it can also back it up. The Bible says that God does not operate on our limited abilities and scope. No, my dear reader, the God of the Bible, the maker of heaven and earth, does not default on His promises. Ponder the boldness in this verse as an added reality check, "God is not a man, that He should lie, nor a son of man, that He should repent. Has He said, and will He not do? Or has He spoken, and will He not make it good?" (Numbers 23:19 NKJV).

"Will He not make it good?" and "Will not be disappointed." Wow! What would it be like to wake up every morning and be on God's team? To go about your day, in all of its uncertainties, even during a pandemic era, and know that you will *never* be disappointed in God and that He keeps His promises forever because He cannot lie. That is a prescription for perpetual *hope*. I do not know about you, but I need this kind of hope today and forever.

Your Hope Is Only in God – Trust It

If you are still on the fence about the goodness of God and His faithfulness, then reread this chapter. Hope is in short supply in the world today. What about your cup of hope? Does it run over? Is it bone dry? What about somewhere in between? Then, God wants to satisfy your soul with hope everlasting!

"This hope we have as an anchor of the soul, both sure and steadfast, and which enters the Presence behind the veil" (Hebrews 6:19, NKJV). Allow hope in the Lord to be the anchor that provides safety for your children and marriage. Guard it with your life!

Think It Through!

1. Have you lost hope today during the COVID-19 season? What are you doing about it?

_____

2. I asked three times, "Where do you go for a lasting Hope? How would you answer that?

_____

3. This chapter shares many verses on hope. Which one stood out to you?

_____

4. True Hope will not disappoint you. Do you believe that statement? Why or why not?

_____

5. God cannot lie so He keeps His promises forever. Do you believe God can give eternal Hope? Why or why not?

_____

6. What would it be like to wake each morning with an everlasting hope?

_____

7. There is one source to that kind of hope. Do you believe that it is found in Christ? What should your response be to God's hope?

_____

CHAPTER NINE

Your View Is Changing – Keep It

What view am I referencing here, you might ask? I am speaking of your overall opinion of life, its purpose, and how it changes over time. I am not implying that you are sliding on Biblical mandates or moving lines of concrete thinking that society considers old-fashioned. Biblical standards must never change. However, our view of life is forever changing and evolving. The question is, what is causing the shift? Are your motivations and intentions yielding to God and His directives, or are your views of life moving in the direction of the norm today with no absolutes? Far be it from me to interfere in your personal affairs. Yet, there must be some provision given to what you hold as steadfast, immovable, and fixed. In other words, what is the true north reading for you as a human being?

Are you moving in God's direction or, are you running far from the biblical infrastructure that you were reared in at home as a child? Sadly, this kind of mindset is all over. Suppose you were raised to be freehanded with alcohol in such a way that it gripped your life and held you captive for years on end. Then when God gave you the freedom from this evil stronghold, you would steer far away from its tentacles and walk ever so softly around those who talk about its pleasure and social enjoyment.

Conversely, you may have been brought up in church and were there every time the doors were open. Sunday morning, Sunday night, and Wednesday night were weekly expectations from your parents. Now, as a grown adult with a family of your own, you think this much religion can drive a person insane and stifle the good life in front of you. So, with everything within you, you resist this divine pull to stay the course as your parents thought best. You may even resent your parents for putting this spiritual implication on your life to continue to foster. You would be in a long line of subscribers to this way of thinking.

Yet, when a pandemic runs recklessly through your life, causing devastation in every corner of your world, maybe you are rethinking this whole spiritual thing. Maybe, mom and dad were not trying to control your life after all but were warning you of the dangers of an out-of-control existence. It is incredible that when life hits the fan, we become more receptive to the Ways of God than ever before. But, my friend, that is a good thing. God, in His graciousness, is trying to get your attention. Life has a way of sobering you up, and I am not referring to alcohol here and then causing you to look upward.

This chapter will not be long in content, but I want to share some revelational verses with you.

> Who in the world do you think you are to second-guess God? Do you for one moment suppose any of us knows enough to call God into question? Clay doesn't talk back to the fingers that mold it, saying, "Why did you shape me like this?" Isn't it obvious that a potter has a perfect right to shape one lump of clay into a vase for holding flowers and another into a pot for cooking beans? If God needs one style of pottery especially designed to show his angry displeasure and another style carefully crafted to show his glorious goodness, isn't that all right? Either or both happens to Jews, but it also happens to the other people. Hosea put it well: I'll call nobodies and make them somebodies; I'll call the unloved and make them beloved. In the place where they yelled out, "You're nobody!" Instead, they're calling you "God's living children." Isaiah maintained this same emphasis, If each grain of sand on the seashore were numbered and the sum labeled "chosen of God," They'd be numbers still, not names; salvation comes by personal selection. God doesn't count us; he calls us by name. Arithmetic is not his focus. Isaiah had looked ahead and spoken the truth: If our powerful God had not provided us a legacy of living children, We would have ended up like ghost towns, like Sodom and Gomorrah. How can we sum this up? All those people who didn't seem interested in what God was doing actually embraced what God was doing as he straightened out

their lives. And Israel, who seemed so interested in reading and talking about what God was doing, missed it. How could they miss it? Because instead of trusting God, they took over. They were absorbed in what they were doing. They were so absorbed in their "God projects" that they didn't notice God right in front of them, like a huge rock in the middle of the road. And so they stumbled into him and went sprawling. Isaiah (again!) gives us the metaphor for pulling this together: Careful! I've put a huge stone on the road to Mount Zion, a stone you can't get around. But the stone is me! If you're looking for me, you'll find me on the way, not in the way.

Romans 9:20–33

On the way or in the way? How would you answer that question today? Your views are changing because, for years, God was in your way! Nevertheless, when a crashing pandemic capsizes your ship of safety, God can now be found on your way, and He is no longer in your way! Funny how life can change our view of things. So, here is my encouragement to you at the close of this chapter:

Your View Is Changing – Keep It

Think It Through!

1. Let's start with the last thought first: On the way or in the way? How do you view God today? Be honest!

___

2. Where is your spiritual life heading in light of the pandemic?

___

3. How would you answer this question, "God has got my attention so...

___

4. Does God have the right to reshape your life on a moment's notice? Why is it hard to yield fully to God's hand?

___

5. If He is the potter and you are the clay, then is God meddling or creating a new storyline?

___

6. Are you too busy to see God right in front of you? Why or why not?

___

7. Are you open to God continuing to charge your thoughts about life towards Him? What does He want most?

___

Chapter Ten

Your Love Is Growing – Honor It

I guess that you have spent considerable amounts of time with your immediate family during the COVID-19 lockdown. What have been the results? I would hope that this dialed-in time of togetherness produced a fresh love for each other. In other words, you realized in a new way that you truly need each other. Little things that get on your nerves or differences of opinions pale compared to a global crisis killing millions of people. But, for goodness' sake, your loved ones are on your side and your team. I call this *team family*! God created it to be functional and faithful to you no matter what. Is your love for others growing? Do you want it to grow? Maybe, you do not know how to love like that, but you would not be alone. I have great news for you. You can learn to love as if you have never been hurt. God shows us how.

Let me introduce you to a list of incredible attributes that come into a believer's life if they surrender to Christ. I am not trying to make you decide on this yourself, but I must share the benefits of such a life. The Bible calls this list the fruit of the Spirit, "But the fruit of the Spirit is love, joy, peace, longsuffering, kindness, goodness, faithfulness, gentleness, self-control. Against such there is no law" Galatians 5:22–23 (NKJV).

Notice what is first on the list: Love! Could it be that a growing love is not natural or organic unless you have the *only* source of all love living inside your heart? Like produces like as the Scripture teaches. You cannot give what you do not possess in abundance. Sure, you can love your spouse to a point, and you can provide human love to your children to an end. That is a natural byproduct of creating a family. However, when it comes to the unconditional love called *agape* love, your cup can tend to run dry. Do not beat yourself over this fact, but rather recognize that this kind of love is divine love. It is sourced from heaven's balcony, and the author is God, Himself.

Take a gander at this, "He who does not love does not know God, for God is love" (1 John 4:8). I can hear you saying, "But, I do love as much as I am able." That is exactly right! As much as you are able is the critical thought. Your love is finite. It has a limit to its ability. Yet, unconditional love has no boundaries or size restraints. Sadly, you cannot give that kind of love on your own. Let me share two verses that symbolize God's love for humanity.

You probably know one already, "For God so loved the world that he gave his one and only Son, that whoever believes in him shall not perish but have eternal life" (John 3:16). Love gives its all and holds nothing back. Never considers the price tag too high for the object of its affection. Human love cannot fathom this kind of agape love. Look at this verse in 1 John 3:16, "This is how we know what love is: Jesus Christ laid down his life for us. And we ought to lay down our lives for our brothers and sisters." That is a tall order. But that is what love does! So, here is the big question? Think of each family member first. Then, move on in the ranks of extended family members. Next, travel in the direction of other loved ones and acquaintances. Finally, consider the likes of your neighbors, coworkers, and church members, etc. How are you doing with love?

Is it growing for each soul represented? Would you consider it unconditional love? Be transparent! Do not pretend here. Would you like it to be agape love? It can be if the source is divine. God offers this kind of love for you so it can flow through you. You become God's conduit of His love to the sphere of influence around you. In other words, individuals can experience the love of God through your life. How does that sound? What a gift to give another human being, especially your spouse and children. How about your parents or your siblings and their spouses and children? There is no limit on who can be touched by God through you.

Let me quickly touch on the other two words in the heavenly fruit: joy and peace. When you have experienced the love of God for yourself, then joy flows from your heart, and peace occupies your mind. Please hear me on this. Love, joy, and peace are things that only God can give you. Nothing in this world can satisfy the longing of your soul like love, joy, and peace. God offers it. You can have it.

Having these things from God lets you offer the following three ingredients of the fruit of the Spirit to your loved ones: Longsuffering (patience), kindness, and goodness. How amazing it would be to be the benefactor of such gifts. News flash: Your family would benefit significantly from such beautiful threads to the family tapestry. Finally, the last three fruit of the Spirit become what I call *inside jobs*. In other words, faithfulness, gentleness, and self-control are things you have to work on to work out in your life personally. Would it not be nice to go up to a vending machine and put in some change, then out pops faithfulness, gentleness, and self-control? However, character-building does not work that way, so God must create circumstances in your life to bolster such spiritual traits. As you can see, the fruit of the Spirit has incredible application over your life. But it all starts with *love*.

Your Love Is Growing – Honor It

If ever there was a time in society and in the home where love needs to flourish, it would be today. Instead, we have a love vacuum in the house. Souls are thirsty for genuine love from their members. Do your part: Grow in love daily.

Think It Through!

1. What does love look like in your home setting today? Do all members feel loved?

_____

How do you know?

_____

2. Were you loved as a child growing up? Did your parents express this freely? How did that impact your upbringing? How about today?

_____

3. COVID-19 changed our togetherness? What was the outcome in your world?

_____

4. God is the source of love. Would you agree with that thought? How can God express His love to you?

_____

5. Jesus died on the cross for your sins. Is that the ultimate act of love you know? How does that impact you?

_____

6. How can the fruit of the Spirit change your life for the good?

_____

7. Love, joy, and peace. Do you have this in your life today? What impact would it have on your life with God's love, joy, and peace?

_____

Chapter Eleven

Your Best Life Awaits – Believe It

Have you given much thought that your *best* life awaits you? Sure, we have gone through some tough times lately. A pandemic can crumble any society at its core, but God is still in control, and He is still on His throne. So, the big question for you is this: Do you believe and are you convinced that your life moving forward still has promise, purpose, and potential? Give it some deep thought. We are prone to live in the past, the glory days, if you will. We look back with a desire we could go back. Secretly, we long for yesterday! A time when we knew of its goodness. Yet, we fail to realize that we mentally edit out the challenging parts of yesterday's storyline. If you are honest with yourself, yesterday had both blessings and hurdles, but we only focus on how the good things played out for us. New

things are God's specialty. Let me share a verse that should make you
want to shout out loud.

> Do not remember the former things, nor consider the things of old.
> Behold, I will do a new thing, now it shall spring forth; Shall you not
> know it? I will even make a road in the wilderness and rivers in the
> desert.
>
> Isaiah 43:18–19 (NKJV)

Friend, this passage holds so much possibility for your life moving
into the future. Why? God can do the impossible in your life. There is
an admonishment to relinquish the things of the past. Former times
are gone. Let them go! Dial in your focus on the upcoming. The verse
above says, "Shall you not know it" (Isaiah 43:19). Is it conceivable
that God can be working different things in your life, and you be
unaware of His activity? It must be so, as this verse is trying to get our
attention to guard against such an action.

God then gives two illustrations that are profound for life-
change. First, God says, "I will make a road in the wilderness" (Isaiah
43:19). Have you been looking for a way out of your desert season?
This scripture says that God is going to make a pathway out of your
dry places. A road provides a way for rescue and a location change.
Second, God is moving you toward innovative outcomes in your

life. Hallelujah. That is so exciting to know. God cares about your situation and your objective.

However, God does not stop there! The final part of the verses state, "And rivers in the desert" (Isaiah 43:19). Could it be that your soul needs refreshing? Would it be a fair statement to say that you have lived in seasons where you longed for a river to appear in your desert wasteland? Allow God's word to minister to your heart today. He not only wants to give you a way out of your calamity, but He wants to provide restoration in the process. *A road and a river are what God can provide for you.* That is fantastic news.

This brand-new life is in the future. Thus, your *best* life does await you. Do you believe that? I know in dark times it is hard to trace the hand of God over your life. Trust me. He is continually working to foster a comeback story. The God of the Bible concentrates on turn-it-around conclusions. I do not know about you, but that reality excites me to no end. Life can punch you in the gut and leave you along its highway gasping for air and relief. Nonetheless, God comes along and says, "Do life with Me, and I will make a roadway in your wilderness and give you a river of renewal in your dry places." Glory to God!

Your Best Life Awaits – Believe It

You may be saying to yourself, "I enlist. How do I get there? I need what the Bible is offering today. I want a path out of my present wilderness. I long for my soul to be refreshed with rivers of life as God's promise states." God does not play head games with you. What He offers, He can provide. Do you believe your best life is in front of you? I hope you do. You can with God's help. Let's end the chapter with a few helpful suggestions from the above verse.

First, forget the past. Please, give it up. Second, behold. Look intently toward God. Know He is doing something fresh. Third, perceive it. Be mindful of God's activity in your life. Lastly, walk on the revealed pathways He provides and let them rejuvenate your being. God focuses on hearts that want the best moving into tomorrow. You can be next on His agenda!

Think It Through!

1. What were your thoughts about your *best* life today?

2. Are you prone to look to the past? Why or why not?

3. How are you missing out in the present by always looking to yesterday's storyline?

4. God is always creating the new thing. Do you look for it? How can He make your life new today?

5. A road in the wilderness. How does that sound for your life?

6. A river in the desert. Do you need soul refreshing today? What would a refreshed soul be like for you?

7. A road and a river are what God provides. What would prevent you from saying yes to His offer?

CHAPTER TWELVE

You Are Now Equipped – Embrace It

Dear reader, as we near the end of our time together in this book, I want to share three words highlighting this chapter. You are now equipped for anything moving forward in life. Yet, this preparation finds its wings if you embrace the following three words: dependence, surrender, and peace. Not just one at a time but in a trilogy of functionality. Let's begin to dig into these ingredients.

Dependence

It is funny that you are entirely dependent upon your parents for your care when you are born. You live day-by-day, allowing them to develop you, grow you, instruct you, etc. This incremental diet of preparing for adulthood is expected, necessary, and enjoyed by the child. They are looking to emerge from the life of one's parents into an independent being. At this stage of living, you are pursuing your interests, desires, and goals. This emergence is celebrated and essential for everyday demands.

Contrast this life with that of a Christ-follower. The Bible states that we were initially living independently from God.

> For if, while we were God's enemies, we were reconciled to him through the death of his Son, how much more, having been reconciled, shall we be saved through his life! Not only is this so, but we also boast in God through our LORD Jesus Christ, through whom we have now received reconciliation.
>
> Romans 5:10–11

We were, at first, enemies of God, living independently of Him. We were doing *our* own thing, schedule, and plan. Through the cross of Christ, God desires for us to leave our independence and fully engage our dependence upon Him as shown in John 15:5 (NKJV), "I am the vine, you are the branches. He who abides in Me, and I in him, bears much fruit; for without Me you can do nothing." The world tells you to live independently, yet God calls you to depend on Him.

The next word is almost foul in our culture. Nonetheless, it has significant relevance in God's economy of doing life with Him and being prepared for anything life throws our way. So, let's examine this keyword: surrender. We touched on it briefly in Chapter 5.

Surrender

We do not often use this word in modern times, especially in America. To surrender conjures up images of weakness. The vast majority would almost erase this word from their vocabulary. However, to those following Christ, true surrender is the beginning of freedom, purpose, and destiny. God is asking you to surrender to His will and plan for your life. In surrender, there is power. In surrender, there is hope. In surrender, there is joy. In surrender, there is Him: Jesus Christ, abiding with you and in you, daily, personally, purposefully, and eternally.

In the Bible, the ultimate act of surrender is Jesus, just before He died in Luke 22:42 saying, "Father, if you are willing, remove this cup from me; yet not my will, but yours be done." *Thy will be done!* That is what surrender can do to the human heart. It does not mean you do not plan or have desires or ambitions. It means that God gets the final say over your life, purpose, and mission. Surrender is holy, and submission is mighty. To abandon your ambition touches God's heart and is life's ultimate aim. Why is this so important to the human spirit. Well, that leads us to the final word as noted below: Peace. As with surrender, peace was touched on in Chapter 5.

Peace

The world is searching for peace today in 2021. Its people seek after it in all the wrong places. Yet, Jesus is the Prince of Peace. When the issues of dependence and surrender are resolved, God brings peace to your heart, being, life, and world. Peace is only found in pursuing God with a willing heart. Check out what this verse says, "You will keep in perfect peace those whose minds are steadfast, because they trust in you" (Isaiah 26:3). The essence of life is finding perfect peace: Not just peace, but *perfect* peace. Many are searching for peace, but it does not give perfect results. Many strive for peace, but the outcome leaves them weary, exhausted, and frustrated. Why? You can't arrive at perfect peace unless your mind is steadfastly fixed on God and His statutes. Yes, perfect peace brings soul rest.

You Are Now Equipped – Embrace It

Whatever comes your way, with total dependence on God, complete surrender to His will, and a sense of perfect peace that passes all human comprehension, you can face it with confidence and conviction. Everything is going to be all right. Your life is now firing on all cylinders, and the outcomes you crave are going to come to fruition. This thought leads me to the final verse I want to share with you from Psalms 37:4 (NKJV), "Delight yourself also in the Lord, And He shall give you the desires of your heart."

Let that sink into your mind and heart. No, that verse is not a blank check for God's activity. Nor is God a genie in a Bottle or a spiritual Santa Claus to be bossed around by worldly prayer requests. It is, however, a promise that once God becomes your delight, that your prayers often become His plan over your life. In effect, you now want the same thing for your future. Thus, you are willing to embrace the direction of God over your life moving forward, no matter what it delivers. So, with that, I say, you are ready! Lean into it.

Think It Through!

1. Do you feel prepared for anything moving forward? Why?

   _____

2. Independence or dependence? Where is God taking your life in regard to this matter? How would full dependence on God reshape your life?

   _____

3. Is surrender seen as weakness today? Why? Could it be giving God access?

   _____

4. Do you live with peace? How about perfect peace? Can you experience peace without God? If so, how?

   _____

5. When you have dependence, surrender, and peace working together, what does that feel like? Explain!

   _____

6. Do you delight in the Lord, daily? Can you see your way to do so more?

   _____

7. What are the true desires of your heart today? Can you put them into words?

   _____

CHAPTER THIRTEEN

Real Life Happens – Thank It

This chapter has much learning for us as we read it together. As people often say, "We saved the best insight for near the end." While you may or may not think so based on the title, I assure you that it takes time and some years of growth to utter such words. So let me ask you a difficult question, When trouble comes your way, can you be thankful in the end for it? I know what you are thinking right now, *You are crazy for asking such a thing!* I hear you loud and clear. However, when we look back and assess the damage, we can adequately record our findings. God brought us through, but He also changed us in the process. In other words, God allows things to get our attention and then goes on a mission with us to bring us to a better place, a holier habitation.

Let me give you a word picture to grasp this concept. Think of smoke detectors throughout your home. For the most part, they station themselves unnoticed and unneeded. Yet, when the smoke begins to billow, and the warning sound begins to chime, you are thankful for the effect of the smoke detector. It signals a more significant danger.

Let us apply that same warning system to everyday living. God positions Himself as your divine smoke detector. When harm comes, God sounds the Holy Spirit alarm and causes you to act, moving you towards safety. One thing happens and gives evidence of more considerable danger. We lament the first thing only to thank God for His grace and mercy.

Let me illustrate this point in this fashion. What if your father-in-law had a heart attack and was carried to the emergency room? In all the frenzy, you would be concerned about his heart and his health moving forward. After doing a series of extensive testing, it was determined that your father-in-law had a nine-centimeter aneurysm in one of the arteries near his heart. It was the heart attack that prompted the doctors to find a more substantial threat.

Real life works that way if we are honest. It is easy to fail to realize that God uses them to get our attention and move us towards Himself when things happen. Could a global pandemic do the trick? You bet it could. Can you say you are thankful for all you learned during the shelter-in-place months? Would you make such a declaration? Yet, in the end, God can bring about beautiful outcomes for our good and His Glory. Read this verse from Romans 8:28 (NKJV), "And we know that all things work together for good to those who love God, to those who are the called according to His purpose."

Real Life Happens – Thank It

God can take everything: COVID-19, home-school learning, work-from-home offices, online church services, social distancing demands, masks on faces, lack of toilet paper, and even the loss of tens of thousands of lives, and work together for our good. So, no, not all things are good. But He is Good! And He never lets us down, even in a global pandemic.

Think It Through!

1. What are your thoughts about being thankful in tough times?

_____

2. How is that possible in the natural? Can it be done with God's help?

_____

3. How thankfully did you behaved during the global pandemic shutdown?

_____

4. How is God changing you today as a result of reading this book thus far?

_____

5. Do bad things always mean bad results are the final outcome?

_____

6. Can God work the year 2020 together for our good? How?

_____

Are you seeing this happen?

_____

7. One last question, Can God change a heart through the trouble one faces? Has He changed yours today? How?

_____

CHAPTER FOURTEEN

Moving Forward with Life

Your willingness to learn from life's hardships speaks well of your character and spirit for living. I commend you for your hard work and the grit it took to keep reading a book, any book for that matter, but especially this one about the unprecedented year we had. However, this book is not just about surviving a colossal year like 2020 but also about learning the tools and truths to celebrate how God turns your tragedies into triumphs.

As you ponder all that you have read, what stands out to you most? Could it be that God was using COVID-19 to reorder some things in your life? That is a great starting point for prayer and meditation. Nothing happens by chance in God's plan over a person's life and story. So, lean into the rest of your narrative and watch what

God wants to do with your life moving forward!

May I suggest that you take some time and reflect on the book up to this point? No, do not read it and check the box for another book accomplished. That is not the goal of this book. Life change only happens when introspection and application converge. God wants to change your life, but He needs a willing participant. I want to do a recall from a previous chapter. Do you remember *trust + understanding + submission = straightening?* Life is way too short to wander through it without a clue of its meaning, value, and purpose (MVP living). God wants to give you a straight path throughout your life. Commit this verse to memory, and it will serve you well the rest of your days. It is true in every season of life. God wants the *best* for your life. He sincerely does! Reread it, "Trust in the LORD with all your heart and lean not on your own understanding; in all your ways submit to him, and he will make your paths straight" Proverbs 3:5–6.

It would be easy to say that this book is about surviving a pandemic. Well, yes and no to that thought. Why? Because pandemics only happen every hundred years. So, you will not navigate the second one in your lifetime. Hence, the book would not serve its readers who survive pandemics regularly as that would not be factual. Epidemics, maybe. Pandemics, never!

No, dear reader, this book speaks more about this theme: how God turns tragedies into triumphs! This book puts God on display for the casual and curious observer who wonders how some people seem to land on their feet after a calamity hits them, suffers little to no bruises, and does so with a smile on their faces. What? How in the world can that be possible with such pain, hurt, and confusion? That outcome is what God specialized in creating.

For starters, every chapter of this book still has application into your life. Your troubles do not have to be as massive as a pandemic to understand that God will not waste a problematic season without teaching you a few things about Himself and life, in general. God is working key ingredients into the fabric of your life

> Therefore, since we have been justified through faith, we have peace with God through our LORD Jesus Christ, through whom we have gained access by faith into this grace in which we now stand. And we boast in the hope of the glory of God. Not only so, but we also glory in our sufferings, because we know that suffering produces perseverance; perseverance, character; and character, hope. And hope does not put us to shame, because God's love has been poured out into our hearts through the Holy Spirit, who has been given to us.
>
> Romans 5:1–5

Let me list them separately so you can meditate on them. These benefits are what suffering avails to the follower of Christ: perseverance, character, and hope. Nevertheless, God does not need a pandemic to orchestrate situations in your life that produce perseverance, character, and hope. How about a troublesome marriage? Or the stress of a demanding job? What about the care of a sickly child or aging parents? Could an untimely doctor's report of impending illness be a cause for suffering? You bet it could. This list can be endless because life has no limit to never-ending hurdles. So, God is not waiting on the once ever pandemic to move in on your life for a holy changeover. There are innumerable amounts of tests and trials in the daily grind of living that give God the framework to flip your life, as we learned in previous chapters.

Moving forward should be natural, effervescent, and fruitful. Do not get spiritual amnesia. Stop holding your breath with fear saying, "I hope that never comes back around here again." Instead, note that life's challenges progress in difficulty on purpose. Before being crowned king over Israel, David the shepherd fought a lion and a bear and finally faced Goliath, the giant. Each stage of growth bolstered his confidence in God and his skills as a person. God is doing the same in your life as well, be it through a pandemic, divorce, cancer, or financial dilemma, etc.

God is relentless in His will to conform your life into the likeness of His Son, Jesus Christ. That fact is good news for everyone who has ever wondered if life is one big test. To a large extent, you would be correct in your assumption. God is transforming your life, little by little, with one trial after another. Indeed, at times, that can be tiresome, but the result is a mind focused on the things of God as detailed in Romans 8:6, "The mind governed by the flesh is death, but the mind governed by the Spirit is life and peace." So, move forward with confidence, conviction, and courage that God has got your back, and He is for you.

Think about those two benefits of spirit-filled living: *life* and *peace*. Any takers? Who would not want life to be more abundant as Jesus promised in John 10:10 (NKJV), "The thief does not come except to steal, and to kill, and to destroy. I have come that they may have life, and that they may have it more abundantly." Life to the fullest is what Jesus Christ is offering, today and always. But who does not want to add peace into the mix? The promise of Isaiah has always been one of my favorites as recorded earlier, "You will keep him in perfect peace, whose mind is stayed on You, because he trusts in You. Trust in the Lord forever, For in Yah, the Lord, is everlasting strength" (Isaiah 26:3–4 NKJV). By now, you should be shouting for joy. Perfect peace is available today! Do you want that in your life? Who would not enjoy peace? Yet, there is a precursor to its offering, "whose mind is stayed on You." Yes, fixing your mind on the Lord is the necessary ingredient to a life filled with peace. Not to mention, the above verses declare the source of your life of strength, the Lord.

Think It Through!

1. What about this chapter grabbed your interest now? Moving forward is a process. How?

---

2. God is always looking for ways to transform our lives. What is He doing in yours?

---

3. How is life like a test?

How do you feel you are doing?

---

4. Your mind matters. What can you do to change your thought life?

---

5. Flesh vs. spirit? Does that theme ever go away in the life of a believer?

---

6. Life and peace! How does that sound? Start with renewing your mind. How?

---

7. Is the Lord your source of strength? What can you change about your life to make Him that resource? How?

Chapter Fifteen

Getting Past the Negative Talk

You do not have to go far to hear all the negative talk about 2020 and life in general, for that matter. Pandemics generate harmful chatter, as you would expect. With the varied benefits that social media affords us today, one of the downfalls of this technology is the smattering of opinions on every subject under the sun. If you give your thoughts about a subject matter, you can be sure someone on social media thinks 100% differently than you do. Furthermore, you can be confident that this person will freely tell you so, and heaven forbid that they get nasty about it, too. So, what is the antidote for such destructive propaganda? It is in two words: mind renewal.

If you do not guard your thought life, then the venom of the negative talk will saturate your mind and pollute your soul. I know that to be a chief tactic of the evil one. However, you have a role to play in this battle. You have the power to turn off the flow of antagonistic banter entering your ears and eyes. These two ports hold the key to censorship as it pertains to your intake. If you act foolishly and open these gateways, you are subject to the sludge of conversation that ensues. So, how do you prevent this from happening? *Self-censorship* is the key to your defense.

Now, before you push back on this needed component of your spiritual walk, look at the benefits of this activity. For starters, garbage in = garbage out. That is a fact. You cannot take in this toxic substance, and it not come back out of your mouth. The Bible emphatically states that out of the overflow of your heart, the mouth will speak.

> A good man out of the good treasure of his heart brings forth good; and an evil man out of the evil treasure of his heart brings forth evil. For out of the abundance of the heart, his mouth speaks.
>
> Luke 6:45 (NKJV)

If you fill your heart with trash talk, it will make its way to the lips every time. Next, your spirit man will be at peace if you prevent this toxin from entering your world. Ultimately, do not be irresponsible as a follower of Christ. This jargon will grieve the Holy Spirit as noted in Ephesians 4:30 (NKJV), "And do not grieve the Holy Spirit of God, by whom you were sealed for the day of redemption."

Another crucial advantage of self-censorship is pure thoughts. Your mind can be the devil's playground or the Spirit's holy ground. You get to decide how to facilitate this environment. If you ingest such crude chat, do not be surprised when your inner man is troubled and conflicted. It would be like inviting a dog who has wallowed in the mud outside into a clean and neatly put home. You cannot fault the dog for making the place nasty if you let him into the tidy space. You are the keeper of the entryway. Be on your guard.

Hence, your mind is no different. Thus, mind renewal is the utmost for your life. God gives you a stern warning

> Therefore, I urge you, brothers and sisters, in view of God's mercy, to offer your bodies as a living sacrifice, holy and pleasing to God—this is your true and proper worship. Do not conform to the pattern of this world, but be transformed by the renewing of your mind. Then you will be able to test and approve what God's will is—his good, pleasing and perfect will.
>
> Romans 12:1–2

There is power in a transformed mind, as recorded above. That is good news for the believer today, bombarded with mind babble from every side. Yet, you have a choice to make concerning this flush of activity. Conformity is a preference over the things of God. No one is forced into this paralyzing state of being. The way of escape is mind management. However, you must take this matter seriously as if your life depends on it because it does. Satan is after your mind, and damaging talk is always the pathway to muddled thinking.

May I be bold here and offer this suggestion today. First, you need to decide what line you want to be in concerning your life with God. Then, consider this verse "Multitudes, multitudes in the valley of decision! For the day of the Lord is near in the valley of decision" (Joel 3:14, NKJV). You are in the valley of decision right now. Therefore, it would be best if you determined what living for Jesus Christ looks like today. Decide today! There can be no more straddling the fence in your life with one foot on Jesus and one on the world. Be all-in for Jesus! Place both feet squarely on His promises and goodness. You will have no regrets over this outcome. It changes everything moving forward.

Lastly, you can edit the pessimistic talk and destructive thinking by doing the following as captured in Colossians 3:1–2, "Since, then, you have been raised with Christ, set your hearts on things above, where Christ is, seated at the right hand of God. Set your minds on things above, not on earthly things." Did you catch that proactive action? The author uses the word *set* here two times, one for the heart and one for the mind.

Much like a doctor sets a broken bone back in place, you must set your heart and mind back in place to God's original intent for your life. The pronoun is *your*, as noted here. You cannot fix someone else's mind and heart, but you can set your own. Note that the words set and fix can be used interchangeably. One could easily read the above verse as "Fix your heart and mind" on things above. In any event, you are consciously giving the essence of your whole being to heavenly matters.

Here is one last verse to end on, "For 'who has known the mind of the Lord that he may instruct Him?' But we have the mind of Christ" 1 Corinthians 2:16 (NKJV). Dear reader, if you have surrendered your life to Jesus Christ, then you have the mind of Christ within your being. Do not overlook this fantastic revelation. You have been given the mind of Christ at your conversion experience. That gives you the power to self-censor the world's declarations and rest your life securely on God's Word and His plan for humanity. You are no longer a hostage to society, culture, worldliness, and political correctness. No, living for Jesus Christ places you in heavenly ranks far above the smattering of activity in this place we call Earth. You are a citizen of heaven, and God is your heavenly Father, and Jesus Christ is your King of the kingdom of God.

With that said, you do not have to try and fit into the world's systems and agendas. Instead, you have been called to a greater mission: to be light and salt. Jesus needs you to shine, and flavor

> You are the salt of the earth; but if the salt loses its flavor, how shall it be seasoned? It is then good for nothing but to be thrown out and trampled underfoot by men. You are the light of the world. A city that is set on a hill cannot be hidden. Nor do they light a lamp and put it under a basket, but on a lampstand, and it gives light to all who are in the house. Let your light so shine before men, that they may see your good works and glorify your Father in heaven. Glory to God!
>
> Matthew 5:13–14 (NKJV)

Think It Through!

1. Why is negative talk so damaging to your spiritual walk with God?"

_____

2. How can you steer clear of participating in its destructive activity?

_____

3. Can social media add fuel to the fire of this damaging pastime?

_____

4. How is God challenging you today to free yourself from harmful thinking?

_____

5. The valley of decision – What have you decided about mind renewal?

_____

6. Set your heart and mind on heavenly things. How do you do this?

_____

7. Salt and light: Do you accept the assignment for God's plan? What can you do to improve this in your own life?

_____

Chapter Sixteen

Let Your Light Shine for All to See

Gratitude: do you have it? Be honest here. It is a precious and priceless commodity in the human spirit, but it is seldom found in today's culture, especially during 2020 and into 2021. God calls these patterns of lamenting destructive. We have all been around the chronic complainer who whines about everything. "My food is too cold. My workspace is too small. My spouse is draining me. My children get on my nerves." You get the picture! These kinds of words roll off the tongue like the poison from a snake's bite, and they are just as deadly. The Bible calls this speech, *murmuring* which means "a mumbled or private expression of discontent."

The wrangling at the water cooler, the myriads of backlash on social media, and the host of personal conversations with friends and family all spell the same thing: discontentment. So, no, your life may not be perfect or playing out as you hoped it would, but is there anything to be thankful for to offer up to God? Can you give Him praise? I bet there is. I would even go on record to say that I think you have a host of things to acclaim God over. Why is this so important? In a sentence, murmuring is a whirlwind of pollution to the human soul.

An attitude of thankfulness is the key to conquering discontentment in your life. Let God infuse your spirit with daily thanksgiving and watch how your heart will always soar with the inner workings of gratefulness. Do you want biblical proof?

> Do everything without grumbling or arguing, so that you may become blameless and pure, "children of God without fault in a warped and crooked generation." Then you will shine among them like stars in the sky as you hold firmly to the word of life. And then I will be able to boast on the day of Christ that I did not run or labor in vain. But even if I am being poured out like a drink offering on the sacrifice and service coming from your faith, I am glad and rejoice with all of you. So you too should be glad and rejoice with me.
>
> Philippians 2:14–18

Wow! Do we need shining stars today among our warped and crooked generation? The answer is a resounding yes, and amen. I shared a recent message at a men's devotional breakfast that included the following comparison. Many years ago, the group Bad Company released the song "Shooting Star."[4] It shares the story of a desiring musician wanting fame and fortune. Yes, he found it, but the result of his life was that he lived like a shooting star. Here today and gone tomorrow. Short-lived and fleeting at best. He died famously, and yet he died quickly, tragically, and alone. Fame and fortune have a disastrous price tag attached to them. It is not worth the exchange, my buddy.

The notable contrast was that of this Philippians verse. Rather than a shooting star, God is raising shining stars. He is looking for men and women who will walk blameless and pure, living without fault in a murmuring society. Can you imagine what life would look like around the globe if people lived their lives without grumbling or arguing about everything under the Sun? What about around your sphere of influence. I do not know about you, but the whole world would take notice of this heavenly shift. It would be miraculous! A total transformation from the norm of today. It would spell a spiritual revival across the continents. Why? Because we live in a land with a lack of thankfulness and gratitude. The culture today prefers to grumble and argue. Yes, shining stars are rare. They are so uncommon, and you probably do not know anyone like that. Chances are if you do, they drive you bonkers. Positivity flows from their very being, and it grates at your negative temperament and demeanor.

We genuinely need shining stars in the marketplace, workspaces, government, grocery stores, and homes across the globe. It would be a game-changer. Speaking of game-changer, I received that exact wording in my boss's first review at my current job. When she hired me, our team had a negative bent, and I picked up on it right away as the energy in the room was draining, and I felt its deadly nature firsthand.

Nevertheless, I refused to allow the enemy to draw me into his web of poisonous banter. Life was not that bad there at Habasit America, but you would never know it by the rantings of each day. I had many colleagues say, "Your positivity is annoying me and sapping my negative energy." To which, I would chuckle and keep on shining for Jesus Christ. Shining stars can change the world. To God be the glory because it did change. My boss said, "Bud, joining our team was a game-changer and breath of fresh air." What was she saying, "A shining star has arrived and filled our team with the presence of God and the spirit of Jesus Christ." Well, maybe not, but salt and light had arrived and changed the atmosphere in a positive way. Salt and light always do that to an environment.

Game-changing and breaths of fresh air are what shining stars bring to the earth. God knew that shining stars could turn over the culture around them. That is our heavenly assignment today. And I heartily accept this mandate to impact those around me. If you want to know firsthand how to do this, look at verse 14, "Do everything without grumbling or arguing" (Philippians 2:14). That is the ticket! This remedy is lost in our philosophy today, but it will lead to a life change in the workplace, the marketplace, and the home. Be thankful. Have a spirit of gratitude for what God is doing in your life. Give thanks to God as noted 1 Thessalonians 5:18, "Give thanks in all circumstances; for this is God's will for you in Christ Jesus." A shooting star or shining star? You get to decide how you want to live your life before onlookers. I choose to be a shining star.

Think It Through!

1. Murmuring. Have you ever heard of the term before? Where?

   _____

2. How is discontentment a venom that bites individuals today?

   _____

3. How is gratitude and thankfulness the remedy for this disease?

   _____

4. How thankful are you today? Rate yourself from 0 (low) to 10 (high). How can you improve this number each day?

   _____

5. Grumbling and arguing? Does this sound familiar around you? How?

   _____

6. Shining stars are rare today? Why do you think this is the case?

   _____

7. Which one do you chose: Shooting star or shining star? Why? Can your life impact those around you for the positive?

   _____

Chapter Seventeen

Troubles Don't Get the Last Word!

Friend, you made it to the final pages. That accomplishment is worth a *huge* commemoration. Your efforts should be celebrated as you seek to make sense of life in the year 2020 and beyond. You may often wonder if troubles get the last word over your life. Yet, I can assure you with confidence that God gets the final say over every life created and the situation at large. Therefore, you do not have to worry or fear that a problem is too *big* for the Creator of the universe. He's got this world in the palm of His hands and your life too, for that matter!

If you do not mind a few verses to bring this book to a close, I read these verses this morning in my quiet time with the Lord. God speaks, and things change. He promises, and He acts so your world gets better and more fulfilling. God guides you, and you get peace and joy once again. It is like the old programming jargon if-then-else. Here is how it works in your spiritual life. *If* you walk with the Lord, *then* your life will be blessed. *Else* you are stuck fending for yourself in matters of everyday living and eternal life. Why leave everything to your level of knowledge and understanding when God longs to be invited into your storyline. He gives you what you need for all of the living and dying. In the end, He is the only one who can quench the thirsty soul. We all have one, you know. I have one. Guess what? So do you. Check out this chapter from Isaiah.

> Come, all you who are thirsty, come to the waters; and you who have no money, come, buy and eat! Come, buy wine and milk without money and without cost. Why spend money on what is not bread, and your labor on what does not satisfy? Listen, listen to me, and eat what is good, and you will delight in the richest of fare. Give ear and come to me; listen, that you may live. I will make an everlasting covenant with you, my faithful love promised to David. See, I have made him a witness to the peoples, a ruler and commander of the peoples. Surely you will summon nations you know not, and nations you do not know will come running to you, because of the LORD your God, the Holy One of Israel, for he has endowed you with splendor. Seek the LORD while he may be found; call on him while he is near. Let the wicked forsake their ways and the unrighteous their thoughts. Let them turn to the LORD, and he will have mercy on them, and to our God, for he will freely pardon. "For my thoughts are not your thoughts, neither are your ways my ways," declares the LORD. "As the heavens are higher than the earth, so are my ways higher than your ways and my thoughts

than your thoughts. As the rain and the snow come down from heaven, and do not return to it without watering the earth and making it bud and flourish, so that it yields seed for the sower and bread for the eater, so is my word that goes out from my mouth: It will not return to me empty, but will accomplish what I desire and achieve the purpose for which I sent it. You will go out in joy and be led forth in peace; the mountains and hills will burst into song before you, and all the trees of the field will clap their hands. Instead of the thornbush will grow the juniper, and instead of briers the myrtle will grow. This will be for the LORD's renown, for an everlasting sign, that will endure forever.

Isaiah 55

I never get tired of reading that chapter because it provides the *best* backdrop for God's goodness and our human dilemma. Can I be candid with you? Money does not satisfy the thirsty soul. Position, power, prestige, and popularity do not help with the human thirst you are experiencing today. Wealth, fame, status, stature, you fill in the blank! You will come right back to this chapter. *Only* God can quench your thirsty heart and soul. That is why God can be called *renowned*. Do you know Him personally in this manner? If not, go to the end of this book. Invite Jesus Christ to give you living water as only He can and satisfy your thirsty soul. You will never have regrets about that decision.

Now, go out and conquer your world. This book has equipped you to make the year 2021 and beyond a masterpiece. Pandemics do not have power over you, and problems do not have dominion over you. Live your life in the power that God avails to you through the cross of Jesus Christ as recorded in 1 Corinthians 1:18, "For the message of the cross is foolishness to those who are perishing, but to us who are being saved, it is the power of God." As I read that verse the other day, I wrote in my devotional book the phrase, "cross power." In Christ, you have cross power today. What an incredible thought and revelation. You are prepared for anything moving forward because of cross power. Stand victorious. Tilt your head back and walk in the position you have in Christ Jesus. You are more than a conqueror, and no weapon can ever harm you. Memorize this verse as we close our time together as found in Isaiah 54:17, "No weapon forged against you will prevail, and you will refute every tongue that accuses you. This is the heritage of the servants of the LORD, and this is their vindication from me," declares the LORD."

Now that is worth shouting about for everyone to hear. The Lord will protect His own and give them cause to rest secure in His love and protection. Glory to God. Enjoy your life moving forward! I have considered it my honor to pour words of life into your spirit and soul. Blessings to you in Jesus' name.

Think It Through!

1. What do you think? Does trouble always get the last word?

_____

2. Why does God get the final say over a situation, problem, or challenge?

_____

3. If-then-else. Why does this programming term have merit in your spiritual life?

_____

4. Is your soul thirsty today? What do you learn from Isaiah 55:1–13?

_____

5. Jesus Christ offers living water to those who would come unto him in humility. Would that appeal to your thirsty soul?

_____

6. Can God claim the title of *renowned*? Why or why not?

_____

7. Forever and ever. How does having God in your life change everything for you?

_____

Chapter Eighteen

How to Know Jesus Christ, Personally

When sin entered into the World by Adam and Eve, the whole world was thrown into complete chaos, literally. The human race was in a *real* mess: physically, mentally, emotionally, spiritually, and relationally.

Jesus Christ is *more* than a savior. He is the one who wants to put your life back together completely. So please don't deny His offer for *wholeness*.

Pray:

Dear God,

I realize today that I am incomplete and broken by sin. The effects of sin have caused my life to be alienated and far from you. I have drifted along without purpose and joy for way too long. Today, I surrender my heart fully and sincerely to your Son, Jesus Christ. I invite Him into my life to give me a supreme makeover, physically, mentally, emotionally, spiritually, and relationally. I endeavor to make Him the priority in my life from this day forward. Thank you for giving me new life and abundant life.

In Jesus Christ's name, I pray and believe. Amen.

Congratulations. You are a new creation!

> Now we look inside, and what we see is that anyone united with the Messiah gets a fresh start, is created new. The old life is gone; a new life begins! Look at it! All this comes from the God who settled the relationship between us and him, and then called us to settle our relationships with each other.
>
> 2 Corinthians 5:17–18 (MSG)

If you have prayed to receive Jesus Christ personally as Savior and Lord, please email me so I can pray for you! My email address is as noted: marvinrobertauthor@gmail.com

For Eternity's Sake,

Marvin Robert (a.k.a. "Bud")

Marvin Robert Wohlhueter, ThD

Endnotes

1. Donald Trump, Twitter post, March 22, 2020, 11:50 p.m., http://www.twitter.com/realDonaldTrump

2. Sinach Joseph. "Way Maker." Recorded 2013 at Because of the Times, Alexandria, LA. YouTube video. https://youtu.be/KeXcHAurv5A

3. Rick Warren. *The Purpose Driven Life*. Grand Rapids: Zondervan, 2002.

4. Bad Company, "Shooting Star," track 4 on *Straight Shooter*, Swan Song, 1975, compact disc.

About the Author

Marvin Robert "Bud" Wohlhueter, Th.D., is passionate about giving people encouragement and hope. He believes that with God, changed lives are still possible today. As a published author and keynote speaker, Marvin Robert creates life-changing content for *real* living and shares it with audiences worldwide. Visit his website: www.marvinrobert.com for more details.

Next, Marvin Robert is a pastoral counselor and offers virtual pastoral counseling via Zoom with individuals and marital teams. This service is available at an exceptionally modest rate per session. To learn more about working with Marvin Robert, visit his website: www.ignitecounseling.cc

Thirdly, Marvin Robert is President and Founder of Way Maker Ministries, Inc., a ministry committed to helping married couples survive and thrive in their marital landscape. To learn more, visit the following website for events and teaching: www.waymakerministry.com As a 501(C)3, this ministry can accept your tax-deductible donations for its operation and support of offering healing, personal help, and renewed hope for married patrons.

MARVIN ROBERT WOHLHUETER

Lastly, to have Marvin Robert speak for your next corporate, non-profit, civic, social, or private event in Atlanta, GA, or in the United States, don't hesitate to contact him at (770) 309-9200, or email him personally at marvinrobertauthor@gmail.com. Marvin Robert would be honored to help your people grow and thrive in life.

CPSIA information can be obtained
at www.ICGtesting.com
Printed in the USA
BVHW061132080222
628386BV00012B/943